Together Again

Written by

Laurie Stephens

Illustrated by

Sharon Grey

ING 4/13 $24.95

Published in the U.S. by BQB Publishing
www.bqbpublishing.com

Printed in the United States of America
ISBN 978-1-937084-33-2 (p)
ebook ISBN 978-1-937084-34-9 (e)

Library of Congress No. 2011945141

Book design by Kathy Papasidero, KP Design, LLC

Illustrations and cover design by Sharon Gray
www.shadesofgreyillustrations.com

This book is dedicated to my
extraordinary daughters,
Lily and Avery,
whom I love more than
words can express.
I carry you in my heart—
always have and always will.

Do you remember where you lived before you were born? I do!
I once lived in heaven with God, all of the angels, and my mommy.
Heaven was beautiful. My friends and I ran around playing, while
our mommies smiled and clapped their hands.

But we all knew that the time would soon come when we would leave heaven and be born on earth. So we promised each other that we'd be together again and knew that our love would make that happen—even if it meant my mommy would have to find me on the other side of the world.

My mommy was born first in America. But after a while, she became a little lonely and began to miss me. She often dreamed of me, remembering her promise to find me so we could be together again. Sometimes, I watched my mommy from heaven, and I couldn't wait to be with her again. I missed her so very much.

Then, one day, it was finally time for me to leave heaven and start my life on earth. I grew in my birthmother's tummy and in my mommy's heart—they had planned it that way in heaven.

But I wasn't born in America! I was born far, far away in a country called China.

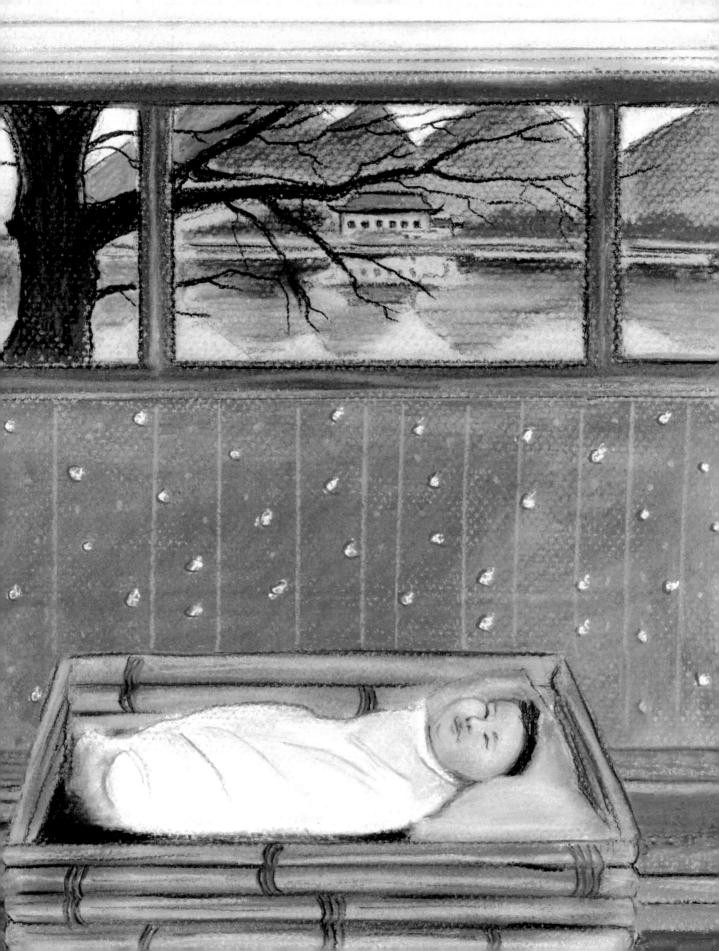

After I was born, I went to a big house with lots of other babies who were also waiting for their families to find them. I remembered some of the children from when we were all in heaven.

The nice ladies called *amahs* took good care of me while I waited for my mommy to arrive.

Back in America, my mommy prayed and prayed. The angels whispered into her ear and reminded her that I was waiting for her. She asked them, "Where is my baby?" Then she suddenly knew . . . I was in China.

My mommy wrote to the leaders in China and asked them to find me because she was ready to bring me home. Everyone started looking for me . . . and many months went by.

Before I was found,
my mommy would pray and
pray, and ask her angels to watch
over me and hold me in their arms
until she could hold me in hers.

So the angels visited me often.
They would make me laugh and tell
me that I was loved. And, most of all,
they reminded me that my mommy
would be there soon to take me home.

With the help of the angels, the people in China found me at the big house and mailed a picture of me to my mommy in America. Mommy was overjoyed! She jumped on an airplane and flew far across the ocean to China as soon as she could. She could hardly wait to see me again, and I couldn't wait to see her.

Finally, my mommy arrived at the big house! She was so excited to see me that she laughed and cried—all at the same time.

She swept me up in her arms and covered me with kisses. I was wearing lots of clothing to keep me warm but no diaper, and I accidentally tinkled on my mommy because I was so happy to see her. Everyone laughed, including me.

Before we went home to America, my mommy and I spent some time discovering China and the wonders of the place where I was born.

We went to the country and saw purple and green mountains, and rivers with boats. It was so beautiful.

Then we visited the cities in China and saw markets, fruit stands, and shops on crowded city streets filled with people and bicycles. It was noisy and exciting with lots of funny smells!

When it was time to go home to America, we got on an airplane and flew back across the ocean. It took a long time, but I wasn't even scared being up in the sky so high.

When our airplane landed, my new family came to welcome me—Grandma, Grandpa, aunts, uncles, cousins, and a big, furry dog named Lucy. They were all so happy that I was home at last!

So here I am—home safe with my mommy.
And just as we planned in heaven . . .
we are together again.